LIVE WYON, British theologian and
riter, is perhaps best known for her trans-
tions of several Continental theological
orks, including Emil Brunner's *Divine
mperative*, and Jacques Ellul's *Presence of
e Kingdom*. She is the author of several
ooks in her own right, including *Altar Fire*
d *The School of Prayer*.

Miss Wyon studied theology at King's
ollege, London, and at Edinburgh, and
elly Oak. From 1939-46 she did pastoral
ork among students at Cambridge, after
hich she was a Study Department Secre-
ry in Geneva for a year, in preparation for
e First Assembly of the World Council of
Churches at Amsterdam.

The honorary Doctor of Divinity degree
as conferred on Miss Wyon by the Uni-
ersity of Aberdeen. In 1951 she was ap-
ointed Principal of St. Colm's, the Church
f Scotland Women's Missionary College.
n August, 1952, she was a consultant at
he Third Conference on Faith and Order
t Lund.

Consider
HIM

FOR ANY PERIOD of thought or prayer
it is far more important to turn our minds
to Christ—"to consider him"—than it is to
consider ourselves. And where will we meet
Christ more surely, as we set ourselves to
seek him, than in the story of his Passion?

These meditations on the supreme moments of Jesus' life on earth—in the Upper
Room, in the Garden of Gethsemane, and
on the Cross—are intended as " 'pointers,'
suggesting a way in which these great mysteries may be approached with reality and
reverence." They make the Passion Story
live in our minds and hearts and turn our
thoughts into prayer.

A brief introduction, the three meditations with prayers, and two suggested "Acts
of Worship" comprise the book. Intended
primarily for Lenten use, it is a devotional
book of deeply moving quality with inspira-
tional value for every season.

CONSIDER HIM

Let us fix our eyes on Jesus,
The origin and crown of all faith,
Who, . . . endured the cross
And made light of its shame, . . .
Take your standard from him,
From his endurance,
From the enmity the wicked bore him,
And you will not grow faint,
You will not find your souls unmanned.

—HEB. 12:2-3 (KNOX VERSION)

Consider
HIM

Three Meditations on the Passion Story

OLIVE WYON

ABINGDON PRESS

New York Nashville

CONSIDER HIM

Copyright © MCMLVI by Abingdon Press

Library of Congress Catalog Card Number: 57-5081

SET UP, PRINTED, AND BOUND BY THE
PARTHENON PRESS, AT NASHVILLE,
TENNESSEE, UNITED STATES OF AMERICA

Contents

Therefore I exhort you, my friends, to leave for a season the painful and anxious remembrance of your ways, to . . . dwell on the lovingkindness of God, that you who are confounded in yourselves may recover by gazing on Him . . . Thou who art confounded with thine own evil . . . shalt surely find My Mercy is greater than thy sin . . . It is clearer than daylight, O man, what He has spent for you: From the Lord, He became a servant; from rich, He became poor; from the Word, flesh; from the Son of God, the Son of Man. What did He not endure? necessities of the flesh, temptations of the enemy—did He not gather and heap all these on Himself by the ignominy of the Cross, by the horror of His death? . . . "How excellent is Thy Mercy, O God!" Meditate on these things, dwell upon them.

—BERNARD OF CLAIRVAUX (A.D. 1091-1153)

MEDITATIONS FOR LENT

"WELCOME, DEARE FEAST OF LENT"
is George Herbert's approach to the season of Lent: the
season of spring, of new beginnings, of new life. In the
same poem Herbert suggests the meaning of Lent when
he says:

> Who goeth in the way which Christ hath gone
> Is much more sure to meet with Him than one
> That travelleth by by-ways.

and where will Christ meet us more surely, as we set ourselves to seek him, than in the story of his Passion? Lent is
an opportunity to examine the direction of our lives; to see
whether the main course is straight to God, or whether we
have, all unconsciously, wandered into "by-ways." Very
often, when we stop to think, we find that we are domi-
nated by ourselves, by the thought of our responsibilities,
our problems, our duties, and even—our importance.
Without being aware of it, we tend to put ourselves in
the center; we then turn to God and ask him to give us
the help we need, instead of beginning with him, his glory

and his will. When it dawns upon us that we have fallen into this state, it shows us plainly that our lives, <u>outwardly so decent and respectable, are inwardly out of tune.</u>

We are like the members of a choir which is singing together unaccompanied; possibly we do not know each other very well, and we are not used to singing together. Gradually, though we do not hear it, we drop lower and lower, and the choirmaster has to give a little toot on his pitch pipe to remind us of the level at which we ought to be singing.[1]

Isn't this rather like our tendency to live day by day, doing the same things over and over again, meeting the same duties and the same people, while we are often working at great pressure, rushing to get things finished, and breathlessly trying to "cope"? Whether we enjoy this pressure—and I am sure that some of us do like it—or whether we hate it, very often the effect is the same: without being aware of it, our "note" is dropping all the time; our prayers are becoming more formal, or more irregular, or more languid. When we are able to secure a little leisure, we find it increasingly difficult to make the most of it; we are "distracted," or "dissipated" in the sense in which Pascal uses the word.

To revert to our parable of the choir: the note on which our lives are being lived is dropping all the time—and we don't notice it. We need a sudden and urgent reminder, to pull us up sharply, as the choirmaster does when he

[1] For this simile, see Ronald Knox, A Retreat for Lay People, pp. 116-17.

sounds his pitch pipe. We need something to pull us together and to help us to screw the note of our lives up again.

That is why in any period for thought and prayer—such as Lent provides—it is far more important to turn our minds to God than it is to consider ourselves. The pitch pipe we shall use will be the consideration of our Lord's Passion. When we consider him during this supreme moment of his life on earth, we shall see how far the note of our lives has dropped; at once we shall begin to start afresh and try to sing in tune with him.

The best way to make this fresh start is to resolve to spend some time each week during Lent in reading the Passion story in the four Gospels, thinking over it, making it live in our minds and hearts, and turning all our thoughts into prayer. The three meditations which follow are simply "pointers," suggesting a way in which these great mysteries may be approached with reality and reverence.

We cannot exaggerate the value of such meditation. Some of us may begin Lent weighted down by a sense of failure, disappointed with ourselves or with other people, or perhaps suffering from some hurt or sorrow which tends to blot out everything else. Here, and here alone, shall we find the steadying effect of "looking unto Jesus" in his Passion.

In one of his Letters, François de Sâles alludes to a custom which he had observed in the country districts of Savoy where he lived. The good bishop had often noticed a farm servant going across the farmyard to the well to draw water; he also noticed that before she lifted the brimming pail, she put a piece of wood into it. One day he went out to the girl and asked her: "Why do you do that?" She looked surprised and answered, as if it were a matter of course: "Why? To keep the water from spilling . . . to keep it steady!" Writing to a friend later on, the bishop told this story and then added: "So when your heart is distressed and agitated, put the Cross into the center of your heart to keep it steady!"

O God, give us light, so to contemplate the Love and the Passion of Jesus, that we may be changed into love and patience. Take from us our selfishness, softness, self-love, delicacy, cowardice, and fear. Give us a spirit of endurance, a love of labour, a love of the Cross, of hardness, and a spirit of courage, that we may be willing to spend and be spent in Thy service. Through Jesus Christ our Lord.

—CARDINAL MANNING

CHAPTER ONE

JESUS IN THE UPPER ROOM

Readings: John 13:1-20
Luke 22:1-34

THROUGHOUT THE PASSION STORY THERE ARE
what we might call "enclaves of silence"—oases of peace—
against a background of noise and excitement. One of
these pools of quietness is in the Upper Room.

The Background of the Story

In spite of the restrained language of the Gospels there
are enough hints and touches of vivid realization to remind us that the quietness of the Upper Room was like
the zone of quiet in the midst of a hurricane. For the
deadly hostility to Jesus—on the part of the Jewish authorities—had been increasing for a long time, till it had
reached its climax during this final week of the Lord's life
on earth. The religious leaders of Israel were implacably
determined to eliminate him. Their only questions were:
When? and How?

They were afraid of causing a popular revolt, which would have been a fatal disaster, from every point of view. But there seems to have been more in this tense scheming and plotting than their fear of upsetting the Roman authorities. They seem to have hesitated when they might have acted. It has been suggested that in addition to the fear of provoking a revolt "there was a deeper and more potent fear—a fear which explains all their singular hesitancies and vacillations . . . the fear of Christ Himself." [1]

When we read the Gospel story with care, trying to read between the lines, we cannot fail to observe that in spite of the grace of Jesus—his attractiveness, his charm, his accessibility—many people were afraid of him. There was "something about him" which inspired awe, and in some cases fear. It was in the early days of his constant companionship with the disciples that they were startled by his power in the storm on the lake: "They feared exceedingly, and said to one another, Who then is this?" Again, think of Peter falling down before Jesus and crying out: "Depart from me for I am a sinful man, O Lord" (Luke 5:8). During that mysterious experience upon the mountain, which we call the Transfiguration, his friends "feared as they entered into the cloud." Outsiders also felt this mysterious quality, and it must have been discussed up and down the country in villages and little country towns, so that even those who had never seen Jesus knew about him and his strange power.

[1] Frank Morison, Who Moved the Stone?

14

And now, at this critical stage of affairs, the Jewish
leaders seem to have been aware of this too. During those
four tense days preceding his arrest, if he had chosen,
Jesus could have done anything with the crowds who had
acclaimed him. He could have roused them to a dangerous
pitch of excitement and enthusiasm. We know that when
he entered Jerusalem on that first Palm Sunday, "all the
city was moved"—as if by an earthquake—"saying, Who
is this?" (Matt. 21:10.) Yet, the religious leaders watched
and glowered but they did not act. They behaved like
men who were afraid; they hesitated and changed their
minds and could not decide what to do. Even after the
scathing denunciations of the Tuesday afternoon they
still held back. It certainly looks as though they were in-
fluenced by an almost superstitious fear of him, like that
which Hanns Lilje suggests accounted for the fact that he
was not tortured by the Nazis, although they were evidently out for Jesus' blood and were eager to find an excuse
to put him to death. It was not until late on the Thursday
night, when Judas hurried away from the Upper Room to
give the latest news to the Jewish leaders, that they finally
decided to make the arrest that night. Obviously, though
his enemies were not aware of it, this "timing" depended
upon Jesus himself. He made the decision, and not till
then did they act.

Jesus and Time

As we look at him and try to enter into the spirit of this
momentous evening in the quiet Upper Room, we begin

to see time in a new light. When we consider him, and then look at the other side of the picture with all its hurry and fear and anxiety, it is as though we were looking beyond the confines of human experience into some calm region <u>where time is ruled by God</u>, and everything falls into place. Time is in God's hands, and Jesus knows that he came forth from God and that he is on his way to God. <u>Time seems to slow down, and Jesus acts so deliberately and so quietly that we feel there is ample time for all he still has to do.</u>

This is because he was living in the spirit of complete identification with the will of God. From his study of the Old Testament he knew that time was in God's hands, and that through time God was working out his purpose of love for the whole world. A New Testament word for "time," <u>kairos, implies that God is Lord of time</u>, and that in the person of Jesus he is bringing in the fulfillment of his purpose for mankind. To Jesus time was full of significance; how often he speaks of his "hour." He has looked up to his Father all through his life, and at every turn he has known the hand of God upon him, and now he stands facing the final conflict in which the full meaning of his life to God—and for the world—is about to be fulfilled. It is a terrible, and yet a glorious moment. Now, in the Upper Room, he moves, and speaks, and is silent, in the <u>majestic certainty of One who knows that this is God's</u> "time," God's "hour"—and that at this moment he is utterly one with God.[2] It is the "now" of the "divine redemptive present."

Outside, in the city, <u>his enemies are busy and feverish</u>. From their point of view <u>"time" was running short</u> and they were anxious and disturbed; they "must get it over" before the Passover, and there were only a few hours left. Judas was urging them on and promising to betray him. The men who were "in the know" were waiting to be ordered out to hunt for this man who had to be tracked down like a criminal, although he had been openly among them day after day during this crowded week. Even in the Roman headquarters rumors were flying round, and Pilate was disturbed.

And then, we turn to the Upper Room and look at Jesus, the Lord of time, and we are in another world, though we are only a few streets away from all the excitement outside.

So while a meal was going on, the Evil One having now put it into the heart of Judas Iscariot, Simon's son, to betray Him, being conscious that the Father had put everything into His hands, and that He came from God, and was going unto God, got up from table, put off His robe, took a cloth and put it round Him.

How deliberately he moves. Without a word or look of reproach, silently he begins to give the humble service which should have been theirs to him. He is doing for

[2] Cf. M. A. C. Warren, *The Master of Time.*

17

them what they were too disturbed to do for one another, and as they wait for him to come round the circle, they are ashamed. It took some time, for you cannot carry water in a basin, without spilling it, and kneel before twelve men in turn, and wash the feet of each one, in a hurry.

Many years ago I was at Oberammergau, and no scene in the Passion Play was more impressive than this one of the foot washing, performed in perfect silence and reverence before thousands of spectators. Jesus did not hurry. He moved as one who had plenty of time. The only person there who was in a hurry and must have been tense with anxiety was Judas, with the thought hammering in his ears: "It must be tonight!" And when the humble action was completed and Jesus sat down again, and Judas had gone out into the night, the atmosphere was clearer. The disciples were now ready to listen to their Master, although their hearts were heavy with foreboding. And his words to them were full of love and peace, and they fell on their troubled hearts like dew on a summer night.

The Secret of His Serenity

His "secret" was an open one; he knew—with a certainty which nothing could shake—two things: (a) that his "hour" had come, that he should depart out of this world unto the Father; (b) that the Father had given all things into his hands, and that he had come from God and was going unto God.

Did he not say: "I am the Way"? All down the ages since then, men and women who have cried out for certainty, for the living God, have found their questions answered, and their doubts and fears assuaged by him alone. In the midst of suffering and darkness and perplexity they, too, have known that he came from God and that he holds the truth of God in his hands.

W. R. Maltby speaks of the learned people who do not understand this "hunger of the human spirit"; these are people who are satisfied to have a religion which is based on "God as a tenable hypothesis." [3] In a recent novel there occurs this refrain: "If one could be certain about God, Charles, we would be safe." How many people would echo this desire. And yet, here is Jesus—all the time—standing waiting to still this hunger and to speak peace to these dissatisfied souls. Spiritual certainties must be spiritually discerned, it is true, and some people are hindered from believing in Christ for moral reasons. But to those who are determined to put truth first in their lives, there will come a time when they will see that all the conditions for spiritual vision were fulfilled in Jesus. His person, his words, his influence, all testify to the fact that there is a spiritual world, that it is real, and that through him we may have real access to God. Jesus himself has said that those who are single-minded in their search for God do "find"—or rather are "found" of him. It is also very clear that when Jesus spoke of God, he was speaking out of his innermost experience; he knew what he was talking about. That is why anxious men and women, as

[3] *The Significance of Jesus.*

they listened to him, felt a lightening of the spirit; they felt that God was nearer, more real, and more loving and powerful than they had ever imagined. When he said, "Come unto me, all ye that are weary and heavy laden," they felt that here was one whose own heart was at rest, and furthermore one who could impart this peace and certainty to them in their troubled lives. All the words of Jesus bear this mark of certainty. He was not making guesses in the dark; he spoke out of profound knowledge—and "the beginning and the end of all he has to say is GOD."

So he is calm and serene. He is the Lord of time, even when his enemies are plotting to kill him. The one reality is God, and he knows that he is one with the saving, loving purpose of God—at this moment, which is God's "hour" for him, and for the world—the "moment" at which God chooses to fulfill his eternal purpose of love for all mankind. At this terrible yet sublime moment Jesus is both our historic Saviour and the eternal Son: "Jesus Christ the same yesterday, to-day, and for ever." As Man, he knows that this is God's world and that the final word is always with him. He is the Master of time and the one eternal and living God.

The Last Supper

There is, however, much more than this in the quiet of the Upper Room. Again, just as he had washed the feet of his disciples in almost total silence, showing his love in humble action, so now he goes further: "Having loved his own which were in the world, he loved them unto the end"—or "to the uttermost"; and again he expressed this by *doing* something—something they could never forget, and something the universal Church has never forgotten all down the ages since then. For from the beginning it was handed down:

That the Lord Jesus the same night that he was betrayed took bread: and when he had given thanks, he brake it, and said, Take, eat: this is my body, which is broken for you: this do in remembrance of me. After the same manner also he took the cup, when he had supped, saying, This cup is the new testament in my blood: this do ye, as oft as ye drink it in remembrance of me. (I Cor. 11:23-26.)

This is what "loving to the end" means: the giving of himself for us once for all upon the cross, and the giving of himself to us—as long as world shall last, for our unchanging support and stay, as our Friend, our Saviour, and our Lord.

To this all the saints bear witness. We can think of Columba on Iona, standing at the altar, and his brothers saw a light around his head. In the stories about Francis of Assisi there is one of a certain Brother Giovanni who, when he pronounced the words *Hoc est* in the Mass, saw and felt the presence of Christ surrounded by angels and blessed spirits, and he was so overcome that he could not add the words "My Body." When he was able to continue, the host vanished and in its place he saw "Jesus Christ incarnate and glorified." In recent times a South Sea

Islander went up to receive Communion at the altar rails, when, to his horror, he saw his father's murderer also kneeling at the rails; he went back to his seat, overcome with agitation and resentment. As he knelt there, he had a vision of Christ on the cross which brought such peace to his soul that he was filled with forgiveness and went up to receive Christ "in love and charity" with all men, including the man who—as a pagan—had murdered his own father. From Scotland comes the story of a minister who hesitated to admit the idiot boy of the village to the Sacrament; after much reluctance he made himself do it; a short time later the boy was taken very ill, and died in great joy, repeating, "Oh! I hae seen the lovely man!" [4] Christ is all to us all, the same Lord, rich unto all that call upon him, unspeakably real and loving to all who turn to him in faith. He loves us all "to the end," to the uttermost, and to the end of our lives.

Prayers

O taste and see how good the Lord is, Alleluia!
Bless the Lord in the heavens, Alleluia!
Bless Him in the highest, Alleluia!
Bless Him, all ye angels of His, Alleluia!
Bless Him, all His host, Alleluia!
What blessing or thanksgiving can we offer

[4] Cosslett Quin, *At the Lord's Table.*

For this Sacrament?
Thee only, O Jesus, do we bless,
With the Father and the most Holy Spirit,
Now and for ever. Amen.

—ARMENIAN LITURGY

We thank Thee, O Lord our God, because Thou
hast given us boldness to enter into the Holy
Place, by the new and living Way which Thou
hast consecrated for us, through the veil of the
flesh of Thy Christ . . . Send forth Thy grace,
O God, and hallow our bodies, souls, and spirits,
and incline our hearts to Thyself, that we may
offer to Thee, with cleansed conscience . . . the
sacrifice of praise.

—LITURGY OF ST. JAMES

The whole life of Christ was a continual Passion . . . His birth and His death were but one continual act, and His Christmas Day and His Good Friday are but the evening and morning of one and the same day.

—JOHN DONNE (Sermon on Christmas Day, 1626)

He said to Judas, when he betrayed Him: "Friend, wherefore art thou come?" Just as if He had said: "Thou hatest Me, and art mine enemy, yet I love thee, and am thy friend!" . . . As though God in human nature were saying: "I am pure, simple Goodness, and therefore I cannot will or rejoice in, or do or give, anything but goodness. If I am to reward thee for thy evil and wickedness, I must do it with goodness, for I am and have nothing else."

—THEOLOGIA GERMANICA

CHAPTER TWO

JESUS IN THE
GARDEN OF GETHSEMANE

Readings: Luke 22:39-46, 47-53
             Matt: 26:30-56; 27:19
             John 12:26-28
             John 17

"I Glorified Thee on the Earth"

FROM THE QUIETNESS OF THE UPPER
Room comes the great Prayer of Consecration, or the
High Priestly Prayer (John 17). In it Jesus says: "I glorified thee on the earth, having accomplished the work
which thou hast given me to do." "On the earth." Nothing is more impressive when one is in the Holy Land than
the sense of reality—concrete reality—which it conveys.
Some people do not feel it, but I did; and I have found
that many others have felt the same—from private soldiers
who were there in wartime to Field Marshal Auchinleck,
who knows Palestine well.

I was in Jerusalem from the Wednesday in Holy Week.
It was lovely spring weather. The pomegranate and almond

trees were in blossom in the gardens and orchards on the outskirts of the city; and even the stony hillsides of Judea were ablaze with scarlet ranunculus and bright with anemones. But the city was crowded and noisy; at that time forty-two languages were being spoken in Jerusalem. The streets were thronged and so were the roads leading to the city. Everywhere they teemed with people: tourists from every part of the world, pilgrims to the holy places, Bedouin from the desert, Jews from every country in Europe, and many others—from priests of the Orthodox Church in their long robes, and Abyssinian monks, with their dark faces and black gowns, to very modern Americans, and "Holy Rollers."

For the moment I felt nonplused and rather disappointed. "Was it for this that I had hastened southwards, through Turkey and Syria, in order to reach Jerusalem in time for Holy Week and Easter?" And then I remembered that this was just the kind of scene which would have met any visitor in Jerusalem at the time of the Lord's last week on earth. There would have been the same crowds out of every nation under heaven, the same babel of tongues, the same differences of race and class and culture. In the first century as in the twentieth (in the period between the two great wars) public notices were in three languages —Latin, Greek, and Aramaic, instead of English, Arabic, and Hebrew. At both periods there would be signs of the presence of an occupying power—Rome taking the place of Great Britain. And as I looked at the lovely signs of spring, I realized with a pang that it was all just like this when he was crucified—that these terrible deeds took place on this very spot, in just such beautiful spring weather, and among equally noisy and jostling crowds. It was "on the earth" that Jesus glorified the Father. One felt the mysterious blending of earth and heaven, of the temporal and the eternal.

Speaking of the concrete reality of the love of God C. H. Dodd says most impressively:

There is in the last resort no ἀγάπη but the love of God. The glory of God is manifested wherever His love becomes effective: supremely in the self-offering of Christ . . . The crucial act of ἀγάπη was actually performed in history, on an April day about A.D. 30, at a supper-table in Jerusalem, in a Garden across the Kidron Valley, in the Headquarters of Pontius Pilate, and on a Roman Cross at Golgotha. So concrete, so actual, is the nature of the divine ἀγάπη.[1]

So when our Lord said in his great prayer: "I have glorified thee on the earth," he was not only expressing the actuality of his outpouring of life and love, he was looking back on his earthly life as a whole and offering it all up to God as a completed offering. But the supreme moment was still to come, in which this offering would be gathered up and finally achieved or accomplished. So before he and his friends left the Upper Room, we see him preparing himself for this final conflict. In John 14:30-31 we see

[1] *The Interpretation of the Fourth Gospel* (New York and London: Cambridge University Press), pp. 199-200. Used by permission.

him facing his destiny. Here, he says, his real enemy is the ruler (*archon*) of this world. But this "ruler" has no claim upon him; there is no necessity to fall into his hands. Deliberately and voluntarily Jesus makes his decision: "The Ruler of this world is coming. He has no claim upon me; but to show the world that I love the Father, and do exactly as he commands—up! Let us march to meet him!" In these words the way of the Cross has begun: "There is no physical movement from the place. The movement is a movement of the spirit, an interior act of will, but it is a real departure, nevertheless." Christ was already stepping out to meet the cross while he was still speaking to his friends in the Upper Room.[2]

The Background of the Story

Now for the actual course of the story: What happened after Judas left the Upper Room? There seems to have been a gap of about three hours between his slipping away into the darkness, and the actual arrest of Jesus in the Garden. When we stop to think, it seems strange that there should have been this delay. We would have thought that the moment Judas appeared with his accurate information and his offer to lead the servants of the High Priest to "the place," they would have been ready. The whole thing could have been over in less than an hour, for the distance was not great, and there would be few people about in the streets at that hour.

[2] *Ibid.*, pp. 408-9.

We know from the story in the Gospels that there was a long period of waiting in the Garden, so long that at last the disciples—who did not want to do so—fell asleep from sheer fatigue and had to be roused three times. Jesus himself was evidently prepared to wait until dawn if necessary. What was happening during those fateful three hours? Judas, as we know, had gone to Caiaphas; and we can see him hurrying in, tense with excitement, saying: "It must be tonight! I'll show you the place!" Caiaphas was expecting a message, but when it came there was still a great deal to do. He had to consult with trusted advisers; especially with those who belonged to the inner ring of the Sanhedrin. All the members of the council who could be reached had to be awakened and told when to meet at the palace of the High Priest. But while messengers were being sent on these errands, there was a still more serious difficulty to be overcome. Caiaphas knew that he had the right to arrest Jesus and to bring him before the Sanhedrin, but the Jewish leaders could not pass a sentence of death—and that was their sole object in making this arrest. The only person who could do this was the Roman Procurator himself. From all we know of Pilate we can imagine that he was not the kind of person to be suddenly roused from sleep in the early hours of the morning with a demand from "these Jews" to try a prisoner. So Caiaphas would be forced to do a most unusual thing—to go to the Procurator, late as it was, and ask if he would be willing to deal with this case early on the Friday morning. It was vital for the Jewish leaders to get Pilate's consent and co-operation. So we can imagine Caiaphas and Pilate—the astute Jew and the haughty Roman—discussing this "dangerous agitator." Very courteously and suavely Caiaphas would say: "Of course, Your Excellency, I know that this is most unusual—but then the circumstances are unusual—would you be willing to deal with this case early on tomorrow morning, so that we can secure death before sunset?" Events show that Pilate must have at least agreed to "deal" with the case.

One curious incident bearing on the story of this night seems to suggest that something like this must have happened. Pilate had evidently told his wife the reason for the late visit of the High Priest; for next morning when Claudia Procula woke up, she found that her husband was already out "trying a case." Instantly she knew what this meant. She sent an urgent message to her husband, who was at that moment on the judgment seat, saying: "Don't touch this case! I have had a terrible dream about this innocent man."

To return to the Upper Room: when the Supper and the wonderful discourses were over, the little group of Jesus and his eleven friends slipped out into the silent streets, went down into the valley of the Kidron, and then walked along the familiar rocky path up the Mount of Olives into the olive orchard of Gethsemane. As is so often the case in the East, the transition from the city to the quietness of the countryside was very swift; at one moment they passed through a city gate and a few moments later they were in the solitude of an orchard on the hillside. The enclosure was surrounded by a low wall. Olive trees, some of them of a great age, filled much of the open space; but there was plenty of open ground too, covered with grass and wild flowers, with rocks cropping up here and there. At the extreme end of the Garden the trees were thicker and the darkness was dense. The disciples of Jesus were full of fear and foreboding; even those who had gone further into the Garden with Jesus were troubled and bewildered, yet they were dropping with fatigue and longing for sleep. For a time they talked in low voices; then they fell silent, as they looked apprehensively into the shadows of the olives where their Master was kneeling in prayer. Now and then they even caught the echo of a phrase. He seemed to be in great agony; but they felt helpless; worn out with waiting they fell asleep. And while they slept, the moon rose over the temple courts on the hill above the valley. It shone down through the trees, making the little clearings as bright as day, while the shadows seemed darker still.

Gethsemane

As we read the story of the Agony in the Garden, we feel that we are in the presence of something far greater and far more profound than we can understand. At the same time we feel, obscurely perhaps, that in some mysterious way this story has an infinite meaning, a meaning which affects us here and now—and one which has significance for all mankind. "Whatever our theology of the

Cross, it is plain that the Agony of Jesus had to do with the forgiveness of sins."

The reality of this conflict comes out very clearly in the Gospel story. The actual words used by the Gospel writers are very strong; they express grief, sorrow, amazement, terror. Some of these expressions suggest a height of distress which contains a sense of something uncanny and terrible and "not of this world" at all. Luke alone uses the word "agony" explicitly; he means exactly what he says—that Jesus fell into a state of mind which suggests a mental and spiritual conflict so acute that it caused extreme anguish, an anguish which affected the body. All the Greek words used suggest shuddering awe, amazement, deep distress, some inner suffering beyond words, something beyond expression in human language.[3]

This impression is deepened when we study the words which Jesus himself uses: "My soul is exceeding sorrowful, even unto death" (Matt. 26:38); the word περίλυπος means literally "encompassed with grief" or "very sad"; "unto death" reveals a deeper depth and anguish as great as that of death, or a "sorrow which well-nigh kills."[4] These words recall the refrain of Pss. 42:11 and 43:5:

---

[3] E.g., λυπεῖσθαι (λυπέω) means to make sorrowful, to throw into sorrow. ἐκθαμβεῖσθαι (ἐκ-θαμβέω) means to throw into amazement or terror—to be terrified, or astounded. ἀδημονεῖν (ἀδημονέω) means to be troubled, distressed, shaken. περίλυπος means encompassed with grief—exceedingly sorrowful. ἀγωνία means anguish (severe mental and emotional conflict).

[4] Swete.

"Why art thou cast down, O my soul? and why art thou disquieted within me?" And they color the poignant words of Jesus: "Now is my soul troubled; and what shall I say? Father, save me from this hour: but for this cause came I unto this hour." (John 12:27.) And all this suffering was intensified by the solitude of Jesus at this moment; no one understood him. He was treading the wine press alone. His friends were heavy with sleep, but he was terribly awake—awake to the horror of the reality of sin. Already in his soul he was tasting the bitterness of death, and the cry that broke from his lips was never forgotten by those who heard it, dulled and stupefied as they were by sorrow and fatigue. Three times the conflict rose to a storm and shook his very soul; and he felt utterly alone.

Here, in this lonely conflict, the battle for our salvation was fought out in anguished and urgent prayer. This sight is like that of the Burning Bush; the ground where he knelt is holy ground, but the fire that consumes him is the fire of love pouring out his soul unto death for an unseeing, unbelieving, uncaring world. This love burns with fire, yet is not consumed, and it still burns so long as there is one sinner outside the family of God.

The simple words of a popular hymn suggest the cost of our redemption more truly than any other words can do:

> Although the road be rough and steep
> I go to the desert to find My sheep.
> But none of the ransomed ever knew
> How deep were the waters crossed,

Nor how dark was the night
That the Lord passed through
Ere He found the sheep that was lost.

All his life long the whole joy and purpose of Jesus was
to do the will of his Father. It was his "meat and drink";
it was the sustaining power and direction of his life, from
early childhood down to these last days. Yet in the Garden
he prayed: "Father, if thou be willing, remove this cup
from me: nevertheless not my will, but thine, be done.
. . . And being in an agony he prayed more earnestly: and
his sweat became as it were great drops of blood falling
down to the ground." (Luke 22:42, 44.) "And again he
went away, and prayed, and spake the same words." (Mark
14:39.) "And he left them, and went away again, and
prayed the third time, saying the same words." (Matt.
26:44.) Obedience was the keynote of his life; this obedience cost him everything he had to give and was consum-
mated a few hours later in his death on the cross.

As we consider him in the Garden and dimly see what
his obedience meant to him, we see that for us, too, the
deepest aim of our life is this: to learn to be obedient to
the will of God in all circumstances and at all costs. And
as we watch him at prayer in Gethsemane and see how
he, as Man, shrank from the final cost of his lifelong
obedience, though his whole desire and purpose was to
do the will of God, perfectly, we need never be ashamed
or discouraged if there are times when we shrink back

34

from some approaching pain or sorrow or act of self-denial. If we pray persistently for courage and the spirit of complete obedience, we, too, will know the power which enabled our Lord to carry through his self-offering triumphantly to the bitter end. A Quaker saint once wrote to a friend in trouble: "I know thee can say 'Thy will be done,' but thee must say it deeper down."

Similarly, when we are meeting suffering which seems inexplicable and intolerable, when our whole being cries out "Why? Why?" and even wonders whether it can be true that God is love, look at Jesus in Gethsemane; wait quietly with him, and your soul will be quieted, almost without your knowing why or how. It was well said by Mark Rutherford:

When we come near death, or near something which may be worse, all exhortation, theory, promise, advice, dogma, fail. The one staff, which perhaps may not break under us, is the victory achieved in the like situation by One who has preceded us, and the most desperate private experience cannot go beyond the garden of Gethsemane.

The Outcome of the Conflict

The story of Gethsemane does not end with conflict and anguish; it ends in quiet victory. When the light of wavering torches comes through the trees, and the rather straggly group of temple police and others come hunting for the "dangerous agitator" they have been told to arrest, suddenly, out of the shadows a man stands out and faces them. In his bearing there is a calm majesty and a great dignity. On his face there is a light which they cannot understand, and they are afraid. Some of these men had seen him before; others had not, but they all knew the tales of the wonderful things he had done and of the strange power he possessed. They stood still. A sudden silence fell.

"Jesus therefore, knowing all the things that were coming upon him, went forth, and saith unto them, Whom seek ye? They answered him: Jesus of Nazareth." Jesus said simply: "I am he." These words were so unexpected that several of the men recoiled and fell on the ground. So Jesus said again: "Whom seek ye?" Again he replied: "I am he." He showed that he was perfectly willing to be arrested; but, he added, pointing to his disciples: "Let these go their way."

In recording this incident, the author of the Fourth Gospel seems to have been thinking of a great deal more than the surface meaning of the words. In his view everything Jesus said and did was a "sign"; this, too, then was a "sign." Think of his words after the great discourse on the Bread of life: "All that the Father gives me will come to me; and I will never reject anyone who comes to me, because I came down from heaven, not to do my own will, but the will of him that sent me. This is his will: that I should lose nothing that he has given me, but raise it to life on the last day." (John 6:37-39.) The same idea recurs

36

in the beautiful tenth chapter, where Jesus speaks of himself as the Good Shepherd: "My sheep hear my voice; I know them, and they follow me; And I give them eternal life. They shall never be lost, and no one shall snatch them out of my hand." (Vss. 27-28.) A little earlier he had said: "I lay down my life for the sheep." (Vs. 15.)

When we link these words of our Lord with the words of his prayer in the Upper Room: "While I was with them in the world, I kept them in thy name: those thou gavest me I have kept, and none of them is lost, but the son of perdition" (John 17:12), we can see how rich is their content. So, at the moment when Jesus met his enemies face to face in a final encounter, he went out to meet them, surrounded by the small group of faithful followers, whom God had given him. "If you are seeking me," he says, "let these men go!" The Good Shepherd went forth to meet the wolf, but his one thought was of the little remnant of his flock. He stood by them to the end.

Conflict is the prelude to creation. As torch after torch illuminates the Garden, as sword after sword comes gleaming out of the shadows, we see the trap closing—torch-bearers, sword-bearers, chief priests, Pilate, the crowd, all are caught in it, and He, the prisoner, is free. To give freedom He must be free, and He is free, though His hands are bound, and the judges are waiting.[5]

[5] R. E. C. Browne, *Meditations on the Temptations and Passion of Our Lord.*

Prayers

O Lord Jesus Christ:
    Who in the days of thy flesh,
    Didst steadfastly set thy face
    To go to Jerusalem;
    Didst suffer the Agony in the Garden,
    And dereliction on the cross.

Who yet, for the joy that was set before thee,
    Didst endure the cross,
    Despising the shame,
    And art set down
    At the right hand of God:

Strengthen us:
    When we shrink from unknown ways,
    Hold us firmly when we are afraid,
    Help us to follow thee without swerving,
    To the end;

    Out of weakness, make us strong;
    Lighten our darkness,
    And beat down Satan under our feet;
    And bring us unto everlasting life.

AMEN

CHRIST EMPTIED HIMSELF FOR US

The mountain tarn empties itself by evaporation; its waters are stolen away by sunbeams; they have not perished, they have given themselves to the sunbeams; and have suffered change, and now in the subtle, impalpable form of mist they can steal up the hot bare crags of the mountain, and invade with freshness its most secret glens, and soon, when the air grows cool, will hang jewels upon every gossamer thread, and bring life to every fainting leaf and blade of grass. So Christ by His Sacrifice for us, by the self-emptying of the Incarnation, acquired a new power of stealing into wounded and sorrowful hearts in their extremest dejection and dryness. He comes by His saving death to dying people . . . The mystery of Christ's love in death can steal into that silence, and fill that supreme emptiness . . . In the hour of death and the day of judgment, Good Lord, deliver us.

—FR. CONGREVE

CHAPTER THREE

JESUS ON THE CROSS

Readings: Mark 15:21-41
Matt. 27:26-56
Luke 23:25-49
John 19:16-30

The Gospel Facts

WHEN WE COME TO CONSIDER our Lord on the cross, again, first of all, we have to consider the bare facts. "The facts themselves are so great and yet so simple, so deep and yet so bare, that it is easy enough to misunderstand them." For many people they have no meaning at all, especially when the facts of the Roman occupation of Palestine and the temper of the Jewish people at that time are taken into account. Attempts at revolt, springing out of the seething hatred of the Jews for Roman rule, were very common. Crucifixion was a usual punishment and a common sight. Jesus himself must often have seen crosses by the wayside even while he was still a boy.

There was the rebellion of Judas the Galilean, for

instance, at Sepphoris, only a few miles away from Nazareth, over the hills. Fiery young nationalists, inflamed by their leader's rousing words, stormed down to the lake, broke into the king's armory at Tiberias, and went out to conquer the Romans and set their country free. The result might have been foreseen. The young patriots had no chance against the legions of Rome. They broke up and fled. Varus—the Roman general—marched into Sepphoris, set fire to the town, seized men, women, and children, and sent them into exile to be sold as slaves. Two thousand young prisoners were crucified outside their own town. Jesus would have been about twelve years old at the time. As he heard the tales of this revolt and massacre, and perhaps even saw something of it, he knew what it meant to defy Roman rule.

The sentimental picture of Jesus growing up among the "green hills" of Galilee, far from "the world" with its horror and cruelty and unrest, is obliterated by historical knowledge. We know—as we could have known all along —that a revolt like this of Judas the Galilean was not a solitary outbreak. At that time the Jews were like a volcano on the point of eruption. For seventy years before his birth, riots, massacres, and wild rebellions had torn the little country to pieces. It is said that at least 200,000 Jews were killed in Palestine, either in battle or massacre, during the hundred years which ended with the crucifixion of Jesus himself. In the eyes of the Romans he was simply another of these tiresome political agitators who had to be eliminated.

Yet the gospel facts, although they are part of human history, mean a great deal more than the outsider can see. They are not "ordinary" nor are they "beautiful." We cannot simplify or sentimentalize them. We can only look at them steadily and try to see what they are. And as we look, we see that they are very great and very deep as well as very terrible. For "they deal with the ultimate things in all existence, in God's existence as well as man's, though they deal with perfectly simple concrete, individual things." [1] For Calvary shows us, once for all, what God is like, and what man is apart from God; it is the revelation of the final significance of human life, of the unceasing love of God for men.

Outside the Gate

Outside the Damascus Gate, at Jerusalem, there is a curious grassy knoll—now a Moslem graveyard—which from a certain angle has the shape of a human skull. General Gordon was convinced that this must have been the site of Calvary. Whether this be so or not does not matter. But this grassy hillock, with the rock showing through, outside the city wall certainly helps us to picture the actual scene; for the Crucifixion must have taken place somewhere in that neighborhood and in just such surroundings.

On that Friday morning the sun shone as usual; but the excitement in Jerusalem was intense. All round the three

[1] G. Dix, *God's Way with Man.*

crosses there were noise and tumult, shouts and jeers, while some way off stood the pilgrims from the country, silent and grieving and helpless. Close to the cross—which was only about eight or nine feet from the ground—stood his mother, silent and strong. With her were two other women and his disciple John. They simply *stood* and watched, waiting with him in love and sorrow.

Near the beginning of the ordeal, in spite of his pain, Jesus spoke three times—each time to give some help or comfort to those around him, to pray for forgiveness for the soldiers and for those who had sent him to his death; to comfort the dying bandit at his side; and finally, to care for his mother and to spare her the sight of his further suffering. From that hour John took her to his own home.

A long silence followed—accentuated by a strange darkness which came over all the land until the ninth hour—until three o'clock. Now and again there would be an occasional moan from the two men beside him. In spite of themselves, used as they were to executions, the soldiers were awed. The centurion in particular stood and looked in silence at the one in the midst as though he could not take his eyes off him. The jeering onlookers had melted away, and the air was very still—as though all nature were waiting for something to happen.

Suddenly, from the distant temple came the sound of trumpets; the Levites were blowing them to announce the fact that the slaughter of the Paschal lambs had begun in the temple courts. At that moment, from the lips of Jesus broke forth that most enigmatic, poignant cry: "My

God, my God, why hast thou forsaken me?" The soldiers were startled. What did he mean by calling on Eloi? Being Romans, possibly they thought he was calling on the pagan sun-god, Helios; the strange veiling of the light of the sun at this moment was troubling them; it seemed uncanny. So one of them ran and filled a sponge with vinegar, put it on a reed, and gave it to him to drink, saying: "Let be, let us see whether Helios will come and save him!" It was a kindly action; it may even have meant a little more than this; accustomed as they were to this kind of scene, there was "something different" about this man, and it moved and impressed them.[2]

The Cry of Desolation

This was how this cry appeared to others, but what did it mean to Jesus himself? That is the question which we cannot help asking, though we are well aware that we can never hope to understand the depths of mystery which it implies. For one thing, we are sinful, and he, though tempted at all points as we are, was without sin. Here, as in the Agony in the Garden, we are driven to connect this cry with that prayer of "strong crying and tears" over human sin: for in the strong words of Paul, "He [God] made him to be sin for us, who knew no sin; that we might be made the righteousness of God in him" (II Cor. 5:21). The horror and the darkness which this involved are beyond our understanding. We can only look

[2] Cf. *ibid.*

at him—consider him—and ask that we may see the hatefulness of sin, our own sins, and repent from the bottom of our hearts.

This cry of desolation is not a cry of despair; it is a cry of faith. In the words of George Macdonald:

The will of Jesus, in the very moment when His faith seems to be about to yield, is finally triumphant. It has no *feeling* now to support it, no beatific vision to absorb it. It stands naked in His soul and tortured, as He stood naked and scourged before Pilate. Pure and simple, and surrounded by fire, it declares for God. The sacrifice ascends in the cry MY GOD . . . . It was a cry *in* desolation, but it came *out of faith*. It is the last voice of Truth, speaking when it can but cry . . . It was blackness of darkness. And yet He would believe. Yet He would hold fast. . . . MY GOD—and in the cry came forth the victory.[3]

This is no imaginative reconstruction; the cry of desolation was a fragment of a psalm (a reminder that Jesus used psalms as prayer, and so the words sprang instinctively to his lips when he could not frame any other prayer). As we ponder over Ps. 22, we see what a wealth of meaning it contains. Indeed, taken as a whole, it covers what are called the fifth and sixth "Words" as well as the fourth. Jesus must often have meditated upon this psalm and then used it in prayer. The psalm closes with the vision of the "ends of the earth remembering and turning to the Lord," and the psalmist rejoices that "to the Lord

[3] *Unspoken Sermons.*

46

doth the kingship belong: Ruler is he among the nations
. . . a seed shall serve him . . . They shall declare his
righteousness to a people that shall be born: *FOR HE
HAS ACTED.*" [4] Is it suggesting too much to believe
that for an instant there flashed across his mind the vision
of mankind—redeemed and reborn? But, whatever we
may think about this suggestion, the fact remains and
should never be evaded: this was a *real* cry of desolation,
uttered out of a deep and terrible experience—the experience of being identified with sinners—he *felt* utterly alone,
in a waterless desert, in a valley of deep darkness—and
yet he held on in faith and cried out: MY GOD!

"It Is Finished!"

For a moment Jesus gives a human cry of suffering: "I
thirst." He is not ashamed to accept the slight relief of the
vinegar, which revived him enough to enable him to utter
the "loud cry"—one word only: τετέλεσται. This does
not mean, as we know, "It is over," or a cry of relief. It
is a cry of triumph and achievement. The word used by
the evangelist is a pregnant one: τελεῖν sometimes means
"to bring to an end"; but its chief meaning in all periods
of Greek is to "fulfill," "accomplish," "perform," to
"bring to completion." τελεῖν, however, has a special sense
in which it is applied to liturgical rites and religious
sacrifices. So here it carries the meaning of the completion
of a sacrifice. Jesus had prayed in the Upper Room: "I

[4] *Windows on Jerusalem.*

have glorified thee on the earth: I have finished the work which thou gavest me to do." (John 17:4.) Now, at the final moment of death he completes his prayer. His whole life was—as has been well said—one "single, consistent, cross-completed act." As James Denny puts it:

Christ did not come into the world to be a good man; it was not for this that a body was prepared for Him. He came to be a Great High Priest, and the body was prepared for Him, that by the offering of it He might put sinful men for ever into the perfect religious relation to God.[5]

His "work" was "finished," completed, fully accomplished, because from beginning to end he was set on doing the will of his Father. He was always co-operating with the "vast divine action."

So the cry "It is finished" turns the Cross, the Tree of shame and failure into the Tree of life, the Tree of victory.

> Sing, my tongue, how glorious battle
> Glorious victory became;
> From His patient body piercèd
> Blood and water streaming fall:
> Earth and sea and stars and mankind
> By that stream are cleansèd all.

Having then accomplished his task, he said, "Father into thy hands I commend my spirit"; "and he bowed his head, and gave up his spirit." He "bowed his head": the

[5] *The Death of Christ.*

word used for "bow" (κλίνω) is the same as that used in the phrase: "The Son of man hath not where to lay his head" (Matt. 8:20): it means to "lay" or "incline" in sleep or death. So the homeless Son of man now went home to the Father, with an infinitely trustful and restful inclination of the head. He breathes his spirit into the Father's hands with the words of a Psalm (31:5)—a prayer which he had probably used all his life, from the moment he could speak—when his mother first taught him to say it in the little home at Nazareth.

As a quiet and radiant sunset will often follow a day of gloom and storm, so now after the pain and the darkness, there is light. Jesus makes his final self-offering to the Father in the utmost serenity and self-abandonment. From the beginning of the Passion to the end the key-word is "Father." All the time he has been giving himself into the Father's hands.

"So Christ being come an high priest of good things to come, . . . through the eternal Spirit offered himself without spot to God." (Heb. 9:11-14.)

The Glory of the Cross

Jesus had prayed in the Upper Room: "Glorify thy Son, that thy Son may glorify thee." He had prayed in the Garden: "Father, if thou be willing, remove this cup from me: nevertheless not my will, but thine, be done." Both prayers were answered: by the suffering of humiliation and shrinking and horror in Gethsemane, by the mockery and torture of the scourging and the Cross, by the experience of extreme loneliness and desolation. They were also answered by the calmness and strength he showed throughout the Passion, giving him power to think of others when he was arrested in the Garden, to be quiet and dignified and confident throughout the Trial; to be thoughtful for everyone round him on the way to the cross and during the last hours of extreme suffering; to hold on in utter faith in God through all the horror of black darkness, and to have peace at the last.

That is "glory." This is the point of view of the writer of the Fourth Gospel. He sees the Death-and-Resurrection as one complete event. Thus the Crucifixion is itself Christ's exaltation and glory. As Temple puts it: "The Cross is the focus of the eternal glory. For this perfection of divine love . . . is precisely what sent the Son into the world." The Cross is not an isolated episode; it is the final achievement of a life of pure self-giving love carried through at extreme cost and emerging triumphant and unbroken at last.

This conviction that Christ is exalted and glorified in his death must be understood in the most absolute sense:

No higher exaltation and no brighter glory is to be conceived than that which Christ attained in His self-oblation, since it is the absolute expression of the divine ἀγάπη. This is the glory which He had with the Father before the foundation of the world . . . But in order that the death-and-resurrection of Christ may constitute an "epoch-making" event for mankind, it is necessary that it should actually *happen*—

that the entire event, death and resurrection together, *should
happen—in this world.*[6]

The Abiding Realities

"Now abideth faith, hope, love, these three; and the
greatest of these is love." (I Cor. 13:13.) As we have
been considering Jesus in his passion, we are moved to ask:
"What response can I make to this great mystery?"

For each of us the response will be different. This is
a secret matter, between our Lord and each one of us.
But for us all as individuals, and above all for the church
of Christ throughout the world, certain great things stand
out; and on the private or the public scale what is greater
or more obvious than the need for faith, hope, and love?
Whether we are thinking of the future of the world, of
the course of world history, of the needs of the Church,
of the sufferings of all who are oppressed and ignored by
their fellow men, of those who are suffering from injustice
and human cruelty, and of all who are blind to the realities
of life, who see no meaning in life or in the universe, or
whose lives are devoted to false ideals; in all these situa-
tions we as Christians are given both direction and new
life as we look at Christ, crucified and risen, and put our
whole trust in him.

Faith. The sight of Jesus on the cross is indeed a lesson
in faith, not only as trust in God, but as fidelity, as faith-
fulness. In the lives of great Christians, and especially in

[6] C. H. Dodd, *The Interpretation of the Fourth Gospel* (New
York and London: Cambridge University Press). Used by permission.

51

those whom we call saints, this quality is always prominent. They endured some of the fiercest tests which fall to human beings to meet: suffering of body and mind, extreme hardship, poverty of the abject kind, bereavement, coldness and unkindness from their relations and even from friends, the chill of doubt; the feeling of being lost in a universe without a solution; failure in one's work; the miserable feeling of having missed the way in life; the sense of being forsaken by God; and the final temptations and sufferings connected with the experience of dying and the fear of death. Yet however hard pressed they were, in the end they always came through. It was said of Temple Gairdner of Egypt that he was never granted any signs of outward success in his lifework; yet as he lay dying in his room in Cairo, everyone who saw him came away full of joy. His faith—in spite of disappointment and outward failure—blossomed into joy: "All songs, all songs . . ." he murmured, and he was "wholesome and humorous to the very last." Bishop Hannington, who was the first bishop of Equatorial East Africa, never reached his diocese, but was killed by hostile tribes on the way, wrote during his imprisonment, "I am learning never to be disappointed, but only to praise."

Harder to bear than even these apparent failures is the inner suffering of feeling forsaken. Bishop Lilje says of a period during his imprisonment in Berlin: "Sometimes I felt so utterly forsaken by God, that I thought that never again in my life, as an honest man, would I be able to speak of the Goodness of God." Catherine Booth, a very great woman, seems to have had a very hard time. Near the end of her life she said to a friend:

One of the hardest lessons I have had to learn . . . is to discern between faith and realization. They are entirely distinct, the one from the other . . . All our enemies have to be conquered by *faith*, not by realization, and is it not so with the last enemy—death? Therefore, ought I not to be willing, if it be God's will, even to go down into the dark valley without any realization, simply knowing that I am His and He is mine, and thus repeat in the last great struggle my life-lesson? Yes . . . I am quite willing.

So she faced death. In what was almost her last message to the Salvation Army she said: "The waters are rising, but so am I. I am not going under but over. Don't be concerned about your dying; only go on living well, and the dying will be all right." At the last she saw something wonderful; her face was radiant as she murmured, "I see," and passed on into the world of light.

So when we see Jesus, in the Garden and on the cross, we know that he endured all this "to hallow for us and to lighten for us all the worst times you and I will ever have to go through." [7] In his strength we, too, shall be able to keep faith and endure unto the end.

Hope. Christian hope is founded on the death-and-resurrection of Christ as the great saving event. "Blessed be the God and Father of our Lord Jesus Christ, . . . through whose great mercy we have been born again into

[7] Ronald Knox, *A Retreat for Lay People.*

a life full of hope, through Christ's rising again from the dead." (I Pet. 1:3.) We have heard much about Christian hope in the last few years; the message from Evanston tells us why:

We affirm our faith in Jesus Christ as the hope of the world, and we desire to share that faith with all men. May God forgive us that by our sin we have often hidden this Hope from the world . . . Here where we stand, Jesus Christ stood with us. He came to us, true God and true Man, to seek and to save. Though we were the enemies of God, Christ died for us. We crucified Him, but God raised Him from the dead. He is risen. He has overcome the powers of sin and of death. A new life has begun.[8]

This new life has created the new community—the church of God—and we look forward to the time when God will bring all things to their appointed end. This is the hope of the Church in every age; and as members of this universal Church we are called to work and pray, to serve and suffer, abounding in hope. For "whatever men may do, Jesus reigns, and shall reign."

Love. "Nails would not have held God-and-Man fastened to the Cross, had Love not held Him there": these words of Catherine of Siena express the secret of the Cross with the utmost simplicity. Those who have looked longest, and worshiped most truly, and tried to incarnate something of this spirit in their lives, are those who see

[8] *The Evanston Report.*

54

most clearly that the whole purpose of God in Christ is summed up in the one word—*love*.

"Wouldst thou learn thy Lord's meaning in this thing?" says Julian of Norwich, "learn it well: Love was His meaning. Who showed it thee? Love. What showed He thee? Love. Wherefore showed He it? for Love." It was for love that Jesus trod the way of the Cross—in aim and intention—all his life long. "His stedfast will and perfect love accepted evenly that which was uneven, and went without reluctance from Hermon to Gethsemane. In the agony of the Passion He sacrificed the dearest treasure of His secret life"; and all the victories over sin and evil which have been won by those who have followed him most closely have been won in the power of his love.

In an ancient legend, Pilate's wife is said to be standing by the cross on the afternoon of Good Friday. She turns to the centurion and says: "Do you think Jesus is dead?"

"No, Lady, I don't," is the answer.

"Then, where is He?"

"Let loose in all the world, lady, where neither Roman nor Jew nor any other man can stop the victory of His Risen Life."

> *Christ stretched forth His hands in His Passion, and took the world in His embrace, to show even then that a great host gathered from East and West would come beneath His wings, and receive upon their brows that most noble and august sign.*
>
> —LACTANTIUS

Five were the dead world's continents
And five the awful living rents
Befell His Hands and Feet and Side
Where man might find a cleft to hide.

O Wounds upon the Healing Hands,
In pain stretched forth to bless all lands,
Be sign unseen in every mart
That vain is human toil and art.

O Wounds upon the Unmoving Feet
Be set o'er every stirring street,
That all who pass may see and say,
"What good save by the dolorous way?"

O Wound within the Loving Side
Press hard upon our hate and pride,
That we may know the broken heart
Alone with God hath deathless part.

Five Wounds upon the Holy One—
O hands of mine, what have ye done?
O foolish feet, where have ye trod?
O heart, by thee is piercèd God.

Five worlds He bears within His Heart,
Five wounds His deathless love impart,
For other Saviour is there none—
And in His Heart we all are one.

Prayers

O Lord Jesus Christ, who, though Thou wert Son of God most high, didst choose to learn obedience through sufferings, even unto death: Give us grace to do the will of the Father with an obedience like Thine, resolute and tranquil, instant and complete; Who now livest and reignest in the glory of the Eternal Trinity, God for ever and ever. Amen.

—A PROCESSION OF PASSION PRAYERS [*]

Abide with us, O Lord, for it is toward evening and the day is far spent: abide with us, and with Thy whole Church. Abide with us in the evening of the day, in the evening of life, in the evening of the world. Abide with us in Thy grace and mercy, in holy Word and Sacrament, in Thy comfort and Thy blessing. Abide with us in the night of distress and fear, in the night of doubt and temptation, in the night of bitter death, when these shall overtake us. Abide with us and with all Thy faithful ones, O Lord, in time and in eternity.

—LUTHERAN MANUAL OF PRAYER

[*] With acknowledgments to Dean Milner-White and the S.P.C.K.

All that we shall say, and sing, in heaven will be of His Passion, accomplished at Jerusalem, in that hymn:

> This Lamb hath redeemed us to God by His
>   Blood:
> Worthy is the Lamb that was slain to receive
> Power and riches and wisdom, and strength,
> And honour, and glory and blessing. Amen.

—JOHN DONNE

An Act of Worship (I)

O come, let us worship and bow down:
Let us kneel before the Lord our maker.
For he is our God;
And we are the people of his pasture,
And the sheep of his hand.

Ps. 95:6-7

 R. *Glory be to Thee, O Lord.*

The Lord reigneth; let the earth rejoice;
Let the multitude of isles be glad.
Clouds and darkness are round about him:
Righteousness and judgment are the foundation
Of his Throne.

Ps. 97:1-2

 R. *Glory be to Thee, O Lord.*

The Lord hath made bare his holy arm
In the eyes of all the nations; and
All the ends of the earth shall see
The salvation of our God.

Isa. 52:10

 R. *Glory be to Thee, O Lord.*

Who is this that cometh from Edom,
With dyed garments from Bozrah?
This that is glorious in his apparel,
Marching in the greatness of his strength?
I that speak in righteousness,
Mighty to save.

ISA. 63:1

    R. *Glory be to Thee, O Lord.*

In all their affliction he was afflicted,
And the angel of his presence saved them:
In his love and in his pity he redeemed them;
And he bare them, and carried them
All the days of old.

ISA. 63:9

    R. *Glory be to Thee, O Lord.*

We behold . . . Jesus, . . . because of the suffering of death
Crowned with glory and honour,
That by the grace of God
He should taste death for every man.

HEB. 2:9

    R. *Glory be to Thee, O Lord.*

And when I saw him, I fell at his feet
As one dead. And he laid his right hand upon me,
Saying, Fear not; I am the first and the last,
And the Living one; and I was dead, and behold,

I am alive for evermore,
And I have the keys of death and of Hades.

Rev. 1:17-18

    R. *Glory be to Thee, O Lord.*

Worthy is the Lamb that hath been slain
To receive the power, and riches, and wisdom,
And might, and honour, and glory and blessing. . . .
Unto him that sitteth on the throne,
And unto the Lamb, be the blessing, and the honour,
And the glory, and the dominion,
For ever and ever.

Rev. 5:12-13

    R. *Glory be to Thee, O Lord.*

Prayer

O Lord, who for our sake didst endure the bitterness of death, despising the shame, we thank Thee that in Thy Cross and Passion Thou dost draw all men to Thyself: kindle in our hearts the vision of Thy love, and make known to all men the power of Thy victory over sin and evil. Make us strong in Thy love and power. Glory and Praise be unto Thee forever and ever. Amen.

An Act of Worship (II)

Behold, my servant shall deal wisely,
He shall be exalted
And lifted up, and shall be very high. . . .
So shall he sprinkle many nations; . . .
Kings shall shut their mouths at him:
For that which had not been told them shall they see;
And that which they had not heard shall they understand.

ISA. 52:13-15

R. *Glory be to Thee, O Lord.*

He was despised, and rejected of men; a man of sorrows,
And acquainted with grief: . . .
Surely he hath borne our griefs,
And carried our sorrows: . . .
He was wounded for our transgressions,
He was bruised for our iniquities,
The chastisement of our peace was upon him;
And with his stripes we are healed.

ISA. 53:3-5

R. *Glory be to Thee, O Lord.*

He shall see of the travail of his soul,
And shall be satisfied: . . .

Because he poured out his soul unto death,
And was numbered with the transgressors:
Yet he bare the sin of many,
And made intercession for the transgressors.

Isa. 53:11-12

    R. *Glory be to Thee, O Lord.*

Wherefore, . . . let us consider the apostle and high priest
Of our confession, even Jesus: who was tempted in all points
As we are, yet without sin . . .

Heb. 3:1; 4:15

    R. *Glory be to Thee, O Lord.*

Glory be to Jesus, who in the days of his flesh
Offered up prayers and supplications,
With strong crying and tears,
Unto him that was able to save him from death,
And was heard for his godly fear.

Heb. 5:7

    R. *Glory be to Thee, O Lord.*

Glory be to Jesus: who, though he was a Son,
Yet learned obedience by the things which he suffered;
And having been made perfect, has become our
Great High Priest, who is "touched with the feeling of our infirmities."

Heb. 5 AND 4

    R. *Glory be to Thee, O Lord.*

Glory be to Jesus: the author and perfecter of our faith,
Who, for the joy that was set before him endured the cross,
Despising shame, and hath sat down at the right hand
Of the throne of God.

HEB. 12:1-2

R. *Glory be to Thee, O Lord.*

Prayer

*O God, who hast exalted the Crucified, Thy Son,
by a triumphant resurrection and ascension into
heaven: may His triumphs and glories so shine in
the eyes of our hearts and minds, that we may
more clearly comprehend His sufferings, and more
courageously pass through our own; for His sake,
who with Thee and the Holy Ghost liveth and
reigneth, One God, for ever and ever. Amen.*

—ADAPTED FROM JOHN AUSTIN (1613-69)
(DAILY PRAYER, 94)